30 Reasons

There's always more to do in life, at least 30 reasons...

Dr. Lynda J. Mubarak

Copyright © 2024 Dr. Lynda J. Mubarak

Library of Congress Control Number: 2024939572

ISBN Paperback: 979-8-8692-9417-3

Published by Rare Books & Publishing LLC - Ft. Worth TX

Email: info@rare-publishing.com

All rights reserved. No portion of this book may be reproduced, stored in retrieval system, or transmitted in any form by any means-electronic, mechanical, photocopy, recording, or other except for brief quotations in printed reviews, without prior permission from the publisher.

Printed in the United States of America

Dedication

Dedicated to my Husband Kairi

You encouraged me patiently and quietly to stay the course with prayer, continue writing, follow my path, and listen to my ancestors
above all else.

For
Regena, Rudy Taylor & Staff
The Community Food Bank
3000 Galvez Ave.
Fort Worth, TX 76111

My Thoughts

I think this second cup speaks for the good in people. I'm thinking...What can I do from home to help someone in need? I'll figure it out after I finish the second cup and my morning walk. I call it sipping, thinking, and fixing. You know what I'm talking about.

Notes & Thoughts

The Man in the Park

I've been watching a little blue car in the park for about a month. The car moves to different
areas of the park when the sun moves. The Texas weather is very hot in August and I know this
person is homeless. I don't enjoy looking at this when I know I can do something. But, what?

My challenge is trying to decide how to help without making the situation worse. Do I take food
to this person? Do I call the police? If they tell him to leave and he agrees, where will he go?
Will they take his car? It's clear that his car serves as his shelter, companion, humble abode, and
protection from the world. So I stare at the car as I fill a bag with sardines, saltines, bottled
water, cookies, sodas, chips, and those cheesy cracker snacks. What will I say when I hand him
the bag? He needs support, consolation, assurance, and hope. I will think about all of that when I
give him the bag. I'm gone.

Notes & Thoughts

Puppy Eyes

Another great weekend was completed!

My puppy gave me "The Look" this morning.

You know the look.

I need to finish that nectarine and banana before our walk

and then have a second cup.

I obeyed the eye signals and here I am with cup #2

and he's eating his snack.

Exercise is good for everything including

clearing out the brain.

The early morning air is even better.

Notes & Thoughts

Married with Children

How are you? I smiled yesterday after recalling a special situation. A dear friend enrolled in college many years ago and chose an online program because she was married with children. Relatives and friends told her the virtual classes and credentials were no good and she should be ashamed to waste money on a 'fake distance program'. She ignored the insults, graduated, and obtained a great corporate position.

Fast forward 20 years. Now, every college and university in the world has a hybrid program in every department and digital, global delivery is normal. Isn't it amazing how things change with time? Her journey was not in vain. We talked yesterday as we shared a second cup by phone. We agreed life is filled with many hidden blessings and rewards that others do not always see or understand. Your vision is your vision alone.

Slow Down, Pause, Stop, Listen

Looks like you have another reserved seat to enjoy this day. Hmm... I'm headed to my local coffee shop to clear my head. I closed the laptop because my crime story characters wouldn't cooperate at 3:00 am. My story manuscript will have to wait until the players speak.

Your brain and your ancestors will always tell you when you need to slow down, pray, meditate, pause or stop during any experience in life. Listen. Listen. Listen.

Notes & Thoughts

Cancellation

It's Friday again and I'm thinking, did you cancel your vacation this year? Me too. Don't be discouraged. Get that second cup, sit down, and create your next itinerary.

Your boarding pass is always waiting. If air flight is impossible at this time, don't forget, the family automobile is always available.

Notes & Thoughts

It's Tribal

Well, it's the first day of a new month. It's also the first
Saturday of a new month, the moon is
full, and you're staring at your phone again. Put the phone
down and do what all coffee and tea
drinkers do; prepare that magic second cup. Magic? Yes. Magic.
The second cup allows you to
call a trusted confidante, special friend, fragile relative, or quiet
co-worker.
These are the special humans in your secret tribe who
understand what's on your mind before you speak.
They pull your thoughts away from the tough stuff in life and
permit you to relax without paying a storage fee.
They listen as you unwind and enjoy that magic second cup.
Now it's time for me to stop here and call someone.
My second cup is ready and so am I.

Notes & Thoughts

Wednesday Promises

It's midweek and you're alive. Alive again! Hmm... Did you know today is a special Wednesday? Why? It's special because you will never experience this day again. You have been granted another 24 hours to plan, update, improve, transact, assist, repair, inspire, adjust, tweak, negotiate, groom, clean up, correct, forgive, forget, surrender, rehab, or share things only you can do. You know what they are. We don't need to know. At midnight this day is going to smile at you, wave goodbye and she is going to walk out the door. You can't call her back. We need to get going because the meter is running! I'm late! Give thanks.

Notes & Thoughts

Decisions

Wouldn't it be nice if we could make all life decisions using three words; Strawberry, Vanilla, or Chocolate?

Notes & Thoughts

Mother Earth ~ Father Sky

Another day in the land of the living?
Well, alright then! Blessed again, you say?
Someone told me you've been paying attention to plants,
grass, fresh veggies, tree bark, geckos, birds,
ladybugs, and other outside life.
Amazingly, we find ourselves swept into new hobbies
and interests by default.
We are now in sync with our Native American families
who never forgot
Mother Earth's and Father Sky's significance.
It's so sweet that we are reconnecting to soil and
the rewards it brings.
Some of us have always been in touch.
It doesn't matter if it's beans, garlic,
hibiscus, okra, gardenias, or potatoes.
Now I fully understand the importance of my
grandmother's garden. Plant it, nourish it, and enjoy it.
It brings peace.

Notes & Thoughts

Sprinklers

You're reading this which means you made it through the weekend. Hmm, another blessing.

Well, I spent two hours early this morning moving water sprinklers. No, not a sprinkler system; the old-school type must be moved every 15 - 20 minutes.

It is a short, hot physical workout!

But, isn't it nice to reach back and do a task using an outdated method, but it gets the job done?

What practice or behavior have you returned to because it's practical, budget-wise, not easier, but it works?

There's an African proverb that states when the music changes the dance has to change.

Go back to something old and simple that works for you. Teach it to someone else.

They will never forget the lesson.

Yikes!

I've got to stop here and move that sprinkler again.

Notes & Thoughts

Digital Directions

Yes, weekend therapy is still in session.
I know, I know. You miss your little, closed coffee shop
because it was a quiet, safe place of comfort and refuge.
Me too. Well, order your java at your
favorite drive-thru and enjoy it at home before your morning
walk. Or make it at home and savor
it until you find a new coffee shop.
We can continue some things we enjoy, but sometimes we
need to modify the procedures
because things change. Your car's satellite system will
always recalculate when you miss your
turn, so do the same for your interruptions in life. Life does
not stop. It just continues with a new
set of directions. Now, review the new map of instructions,
obey the construction signs, stay in
your lane, and drive safely.

Notes & Thoughts

Rescue Me

Good morning family and friends!

All is well with me.

If you are retired or work from home you

are looking at the clock, peeking out the window, deciding to

start or skip that morning walk,

changing TV channels, wondering about your checking

account, or staring at your cell phone.

If I know you like I think I know you,

you are doing all of it.

While making those big, groundbreaking decisions make

sure to create some time and space for yourself.

Spend an hour focusing on yourself instead of saving

someone else or saving the world.

I know. It's hard, but do it!

Friday Reminder

If you were blessed enough to wake up and read this you already know it's Friday. I believe we all have stories, don't we? Your life is a series and every episode is important.

Tweak your role each week, support the other characters if possible, and leave the viewers with a message of hope.

And, it's still OK to rest before the director says 'action.'

Weekend Mornings

Good morning.

Are you sipping that smooth cup of coffee or tea?

Are you going to walk before

the Texas sun says you waited too long? Let's encourage

each other, water those plants, stay

positive, and it won't hurt if you take a news break, again.

You know the adage,

"No news is good news."

We can do this!

Notes & Thoughts

Reset your Thermostat

Yesterday was rough. My home A/C died and the tech finished at 9:40 last night.

In addition, I didn't drink enough water and I forgot to take my turmeric. I said all that to say rise and shine, do your best, help each other, and get it done no matter how badly it hurts because it requires your attention.

Today is a new day.

All is well again. Let's get going!

My coffee and your tea are calling!

Ice Cream Anonymous

I have an allergy test scheduled for next week. After all the itching, sneezing, and coughing I decided it was time. My doctor said protect yourself from everything until we can figure this out. This morning I put on my "3 layered mask", surgical gloves, medical face shield, urban turban, knee-high cotton socks, certified combat boots, sanitizer, disinfectant spray (in my car cup holder), and went to the local supermarket. I was protected from the shoppers, display cases, free food samples, the big, steel supermarket door handle, shopping carts, and the evil, self-help, scan everything-yourself register. I came home with enough ice cream to supply every home in Fort Worth, TX. I need to join Ice Cream Anonymous. Don't judge.

Notes & Thoughts

Little Things

Isn't it wonderful to wake up at home and not in the ICU? Hmm... I will be very honest about this morning. This was not a "Ms. Goody 2 Shoes Day" for me. I made up my mind at 5:30 am that I was not going to deal with oatmeal or bran cereal. Nooo, not today. I walked into my kitchen, prepared that famous, second cup of coffee, and devoured three brownies. My arteries will just have to get over it today. Sometimes it's nice to be nice to yourself. Am I abandoning my fat-free diet? No. Have I given up on eating nutritious meals? No. I just needed to relax for a few minutes. Hush.
Yes, there are times in this life when you need to enjoy the tiny things, events, and moments that refresh your spirit. It may be a phone call from a relative, an update on your partner's health condition, or a bowl of your mother's mouth-watering peach cobbler. Do it, relish it, and return to your regularly, scheduled daily program. If it's food, don't forget to smile as you take the last bite, spoonful, or sip.

The Trouble With Apps

Are you pouring that second cup? The past week has been very interesting for me. I told a
classmate I think I need an app that tells me why I walked into a room. I've been blaming this on
aging, but I have younger friends and associates who are experiencing the same challenge. Oh
no, you too? We are all surrounded by too many "Apps" in various forms and categories that
operate 24/7. As a result, we are overrun with alerts, warnings, updates, recalls, forecasts,
predictions, opinions, mandates, and special reports.
If this is true, I need to remember that the
greatest 'App' is my brain and I need to treat it like my cell phone. You know the routine; delete
some programs, turn off the power for a while, and free up some memory.
Now, why am I standing in the hallway?
Why? The coffee is in the kitchen.
The passwords have
fried my brain.

Old School

Remember your grandparents and their lifestyle? Their food
was not thrown away.
Everything had a place in today's meal,
the next meal, or dessert.
Sour milk was not discarded.
It was saved to make cornbread.
Old bread was not thrown away.
It was used to make bread pudding and
dressing, or you fed it to the birds.
There was no commercial pet food.
Every plate was scraped clean.
Your cat or puppy ate 'scraps' from the table,
but never chicken bones.
Mason jars were used for storage, canning, drinking glasses,
and catching bugs.
Ahh, I miss those days and the
lightning bugs; fire fires to you city folks.

Notes & Thoughts

Personal Project

At some time in life, you need a personal project that has
meaning for you, only.
No spouse, partner, sibling, child, in-law, or coworker
should have a part in this.
Their opinions are not essential in this special
experience.
You must work on the project alone,
in your own space, at
your own time.
If you choose to present it later; be wise.
Many times a personal project is best
when it remains personal.

Message to an Old Friend

I was startled yesterday when I discovered an email message to an old friend on my computer.
She was sweet, my confidant, and an inspiration for many years. I cried when I looked at the date
of the email. She passed six years ago and the message was still on the sent page of my
computer. I wonder how I will be received and regarded when my passing is re-visited in an old
email, sympathy card, canceled check, or voice mail. Only time will tell.

Notes & Thoughts

Reality Check

If you need a reality check, visit the Grand Canyon, an
Indian reservation, a memory care
facility, or do a plantation tour.
Whatever, whoever, you think you are; you are not.
These visits will put you back in your place, leave you
breathless, and remind you that you play a small role
in a huge creation.
The experience will also let you know
you are not the director in this production.
What a relief.
Thank God!

Notes & Thoughts

Competition

The conversations always begin with pleasantries and then it begins. The constant need to
discredit co-workers, and devalue family and friends is now in full gear. After years of chatting
with this person, it suddenly dawns on me that I am conversing with a fierce competitor of
anyone and everyone. This is my last day to endure the pain and take the bullets from someone
else's strange addiction to be bigger and better than anyone available. If this person calls again, I
cannot, will not answer. I have finally learned that being accommodating and tolerant of others
also requires boundaries. I should have stopped the strange conversations years ago, but being an
accommodator I allowed the behavior to blossom. And, if I participated in the conversations
along the way, I was also part of the problem. Competitors never stop competing.
Slow learners learn, slowly...

Kindness

My Granny always said "Be nice to people, Lynda.

You never know who's going to have to give

you a cold cup of water."

People remember when you were mean to them.

In the end, they don't

care why you were mean.

They just remember that you were.

Notes & Thoughts

Sponsorship

People will tell you who they are if you listen long enough.

When they talk, talk, talk, and end

the conversations with "...as long as I don't have to be out of

anything," it is a red flag.

Be warned and aware they want the best life has to offer as

long as it is sponsored by someone else.

Change Lamps or Change Rooms

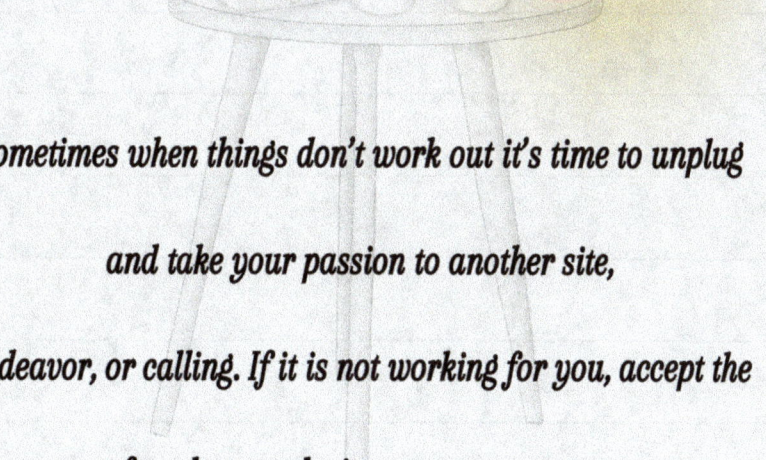

Sometimes when things don't work out it's time to unplug and take your passion to another site, endeavor, or calling. If it is not working for you, accept the fact that maybe it was not meant to be or be everlasting. Lamps sometimes look better in another room in the same house.

Total Recall

*I have an associate who seems to enjoy telling me and
anyone who listens how she has to
instruct others constantly and it makes me very
uncomfortable. Why must you broadcast your
assistance to a coworker, family member, or friend? I have
finally decided that it's not good to
declare or boast with "I had to show so and so how to do
such and such." After all, someone
along the way taught you and me.
Remember? Remember?*

Notes & Thoughts

At Last

At some early period in your life, you looked at your elders
while silently and privately calling
them "old people" who talked about how things used to be
and should be right now. You giggled
and went about your way. Then, you awoke one day and
realized you are now in that select
group of the population who have more medications in the
bathroom cabinet than shoes in the
closet. In addition, there are scheduled doctor's
appointments monthly or weekly, and the refills
for prescriptions increase. Wow! Now you need to adjust
your reading glasses on your nose
before you read the next paragraph. Lastly, you can't find
your cell phone or keys unless you are
committed to putting them in the same place, on the same
table, next to the same door.
You have
arrived.
At last.

Notes & Thoughts

Choose Two

One of the most difficult things to do in life is to clean the house or room of a deceased relative or friend. You sort, you stare, and you walk away to come back again and repeat. What do I discard? What do I keep? What do I give to another relative or friend? I have been told to try an old rule of "select two" and give up the rest. How do you summarize the life of a human being in two pieces? Every piece has its own story. I'm overwhelmed, but I'm going to follow the rules to deal with my grief and life experiences. Now, which two?
Help me, Lord.

Dr. Lynda J. Mubarak is an award-winning
children's book author,
former educator and
Army veteran. She has served as a Crisis Intervention
and Dyslexia teacher, literacy
advocate and new author mentor.
She is a graduate of Texas Christian University,
Texas Wesleyan University and Nova SE University.
Dr. Mubarak strongly believes
community service should be a continuous part
of the education process from early
childhood through high school to include university
or tech school training. Dr. Lynda
enjoys travel, vintage movies, crossword competitions,
and long walks with her dog, Shorty Junior.

Notes & Thoughts

www.ingramcontent.com/pod-product-compliance
Lightning Source LLC
LaVergne TN
LVHW022001060526
838201LV00048B/1647